James W. Humphrey

Manual of Reading

For Use in Normal Classes and Graded and Common Schools

James W. Humphrey

Manual of Reading
For Use in Normal Classes and Graded and Common Schools

ISBN/EAN: 9783337780128

Printed in Europe, USA, Canada, Australia, Japan

Cover: Foto ©Thomas Meinert / pixelio.de

More available books at **www.hansebooks.com**

MANUAL

OF

READING,

FOR USE IN

NORMAL CLASSES

AND

Graded and Common Schools.

BY J. W. HUMPHREY,

Author of Review Diagrams of U. S. History,
Civil Government, Geography, Reading,
Arithmetic, Physiology, and
Penmanship.

WAYLAND, MICH :
PUBLISHED BY THE AUTHOR.
1885.

PREFACE.

We issue this little Manual of Reading in order to supply those desiring to review with exercises sufficiently complete for a thorough drill in all the elements of the art, and at a price within the reach of all.

By general consent no subject taught in our schools is more important and none in which the instruction is more vague and unprofitable.

In other branches of study the teacher points the way without hesitation ; the rule to be followed is plainly marked out, but in reading, too often, the pupil is left without a guide, *to read as he talks*, and to grope his way in the dark with uncertainty. If teacher and pupil shall find something here to awaken a greater interest in this much neglected study and at the same time offer means for its thorough review, we shall feel fully repaid for its preparation.

We gratefully acknowledge our indebtedness to Messrs. Houghton, Mifflin & Co., of Boston, for permission to use selections from their copyrighted· works.

To the leading educational publishing houses for the aid received from their series of readers, which we often consulted, to our educational journals for selections, and to many of our fellow teachers for valuable suggestions, the thanks of the author are due.

λ

LESSON I.

1. Reading is the perusal or the oral expression of written or printed composition.

2. The two objects of reading are (1) to gain and (2) to impart knowledge.

3. The proper expression of thought in reading requires (1) that the reader shall have a clear concept of the meaning to be conveyed by the author, and (2) that he shall be able to impart that meaning to others.

4. Good reading requires that the reader shall have (1) a correct idea of the pronunciation and meaning of words ; (2) that he shall understand the meaning of the author ; (3) that he shall know what expression is required, and (4) that he shall be able to deliver the sentiment correctly,

5. A knowledge of *orthoepy, expression* and *gesture* are essential in reading.

6. *Orthoepy* or *correct pronunciation* is the proper utterance of words.

7. *Expression* is the conveyance of thought by the modulated voice.

8. *Gesture* is action or attitude used to express or enforce sentiment or emotion.

QUESTIONS.

1. What is reading ?
2. What are the objects of reading ?
3. What is necessary to proper expression in reading ?
4. What does good reading require ?
5. What is essential in reading ?
6. What is orthoepy ?
7. What is expression ?
8. What is gesture ?

LESSON II.

ORTHOEPY.

1. *Orthoepy* includes *articulation, syllabication* and *accent.*

2. *Articulation* is the utterance of the elementary sounds separately or combined.

3. To acquire a correct articulation it is necessary (1) to have an accurate knowledge of the elementary sounds ; (2) to know the appropriate places for these sounds in words, and (3) to apply this knowledge constantly in reading and conversation.

4. Each elementary sound, syllable and word should be uttered distinctly.

5. The organs of speech are the lips, teeth, tongue and palate.

6. The voice is produced by the passage of air through the Larynx.

7. The elementary sounds are divided into *vocals, sub-vocals* and *aspirates.*

8. *Vocals* are those tones of voice which are unobstructed by the organs of speech.

9. *Sub-vocals* are those tones of voice which are modulated by the organs of speech.

10. *Aspirates* are those elementary sounds which are produced by the breath alone.

11. The principal errors in Articulation to be avoided are (1) the addition of one or more elementary sounds ; as elum for elm. (2) The omission of one or more elementary sounds ; as trav'ler for traveler, and (3) the using of one elementary sound for another ; as set for sit.

QUESTIONS.

1. What does orthoepy include ?
2. What is articulation ?
3. How is a correct articulation acquired ?
4. How should each elementary sound, syllable and word be uttered ?
5. Name the organs of speech.
6. How is the voice produced ?
7. How are the elementary sounds divided ?
8. What are vocals ?
9. What are sub-vocals ?
10. What are aspirates ?
11. Name the principal errors in articulation.

Practice on the following selections in articulation :

1. The bold, blustering boys broke bolts and bars.
2. I will instruct thee and teach thee in the way which thou shouldst go.
3. She shuns sunshine ; do you shun sunshine ?
4. The battle is not to the strong alone ; it is to the vigilant, the active, the brave.

5.   Whispers of revenge passed silently around among the troops.

6.   Masses of immense magnitude move majestically through the vast empire of the solar system.

7.   He adds thirds, fourths, fifths, sixths and sevenths rapidly.

8.   While he delights in enterprise and action, and the stronger energies of the soul, she is led to engage in calmer pursuits, and seek for gentler employment.

9.   Take the wings
   Of the morning, and the Barcan desert pierce ;
   Or lose thyself in the continuous woods
   Where rolls the Oregon, and hears no sound,
   Save his own dashing ; yet the dead are there ;
   And millions in those solitudes, since first
   The flight of years began, have laid them down
   In their last sleep.

10.   While that venerated instrument shall continue to exist ; while its sacred spirit shall dwell with the people of this nation, or the free institutions that have grown out of it, be preserved and respected ; our children and our children's children, to the latest generation, will bless the names of these illustrious benefactors, and cherish their memory with reverential respect.

11.   Could the genius of our country reveal to our astonished view the future glories which await the progress of confederated America ; could he show us the countless millions who will swarm in the wide-spread valleys of the west, tasting of happiness and sharing the blessings of equal laws ; could he unroll the pages of her history, and permit us to see the fierce struggles of her factions, the rapid mutations of her empire, the bloody fields of her triumphs and her disasters ; could he crowd these awful visions upon our souls ; we should see that all

the prosperity that awaits us depends on the supremacy of mind, on the cultivation of intellect, on the diffusion of knowledge and the arts.

12.—

To him, who in the love of nature holds
Communion with her visible forms, she speaks
A various language ; for his gayer hours
She has a voice of gladness, and a smile
And eloquence of beauty ; and she glides
Into his darker musings, with a mild
And gentle sympathy, that steals away
Their sharpness, ere he is aware.

LESSON III.

SYLLABICATION.

1. Syllabication is the process of dividing words into syllables.

2. A syllable is one or more elementary sounds uttered in unison.

3. A word of one syllable is called a monosyllable.

4. A word of two syllables is called a dissyllable.

5. A word of three syllables is called a trisyllable.

6. A word of four or more syllables is called a polysyllable.

7. The last syllable of a word is called the *ultimate*.

8. The last syllable of a word but one is called the *penult*.

9. The last syllable of a word but two is called the *antepenult*.

10. The last syllable of a word but three is called the *preantepenult*.

11. Words have as many syllables as they contain vowel sounds.

12. The consonants of a word belong to some vowel and are antecedent to it when they go before it, and consequent when they follow it.

13. A syllable should never be divided at the end of a line.

14. ⁀Constant use of the dictionary should be made in the study of syllabication.

QUESTIONS.

1. What is syllabication?
2. What is a syllable?
3. What is a monosyllable?
4. What is a dissyllable?
5. What is a trisyllable?
6. What is a polysyllable?
7. What is the ultimate?
8. What is the penult?
9. What is the antepenult?
10. What is the preantepenult?
11. How many syllables have words?
12. To what does a consonant belong?
13. How should a word be divided at the end of a line?
14. How should the dictionary be used?

Syllabicate the following words giving the number and the names of the syllables: violate, possibility, impertinent, affinity, conversant, series, dauntless, multitudinous, realm, truthfulness, suppressed, revel, given, cession, canvass, excellence, military, furlough, aggrieve.

brevier, chrysalis, basilisk, caterpiller, permeate, parachute, martyr, orchestra, qualm, usurp, utilize, cleanliness, superfluous, stupendous, velveteen, criticism, envelope, lattice, vacillate, paucity, oscillate, scintillate, tenacity.

LESSON IV.

ACCENT.

1. Accent is a more forcible stress of voice upon one syllable of a word than upon another.

2. The *primary accent* is the more forcible stress of voice.

3. The *secondary accent* is the less forcible stress of voice.

4. Unaccented syllables should be uttered distinctly.

5. Dissyllables admit of no general rule of *accentuation*.

6. Trisyllables and polysyllables, derived from dissyllables, usually retain the accent of their primitives.

7. Participles retain the accent of their verbs.

8. Words from the Greek or Latin retain the accent of the original.

9. Words having the same orthography are usually distinguished by a difference in accent.

10. Accent is often transferred from one syllable to another to express opposition of meaning.

11. The *primary accent* is indicated by the acute, and the *secondary* by the grave.

NOTE.—In Webster's dictionary the principal accent is indicated by a heavy mark, and the secondary accent by a lighter mark; these marks also indicate the division of words into syllables.

QUESTIONS.

1. What is accent?
2. What is the primary accent?
3. What is the secondary accent?
4. What is said of unaccented syllables?
5. What is sald of the accentuation of dissyllables?
6. How are trisyllables and polysyllables accented?
7. How are participles accented?
8. What is said of the accentuation of Greek and Latin words?
9. How are words of the same orthography accented?
10. What is said of the change of accent?
11. How is accent indicated?

Accentuate and mark diacritically the following words: Commercial, christian, avaricious, aversion, perfume, impropriety, converse, conflict, economy, narrative, relinquish, convalescent, orthoepy, aqueous, recipient, exorbitant, descendant, quinine, oasis, dessert, elicit, facility, mercenary, stereotype, stigmatize, supervise, systematize, advertise, civilize, aggrandize, patronize, secrecy, controversy, heroism, finance, horizon, hygiene.

To the Teacher.---Take selections from the reading lessons as additional exercises upon syllabication and accentuation.

LESSON V.

EXPRESSION.

1. Expression includes modulation, emphasis, personation, pauses, slur and monotone.

MODULATION.

2. Modulation is the variation of voice heard in reading and speaking, and includes *pitch, rate, quality, quantity, stress* and *inflection.*

3. *Pitch* or *key* has reference to the elevation of the voice, as heard in reading and speaking.

4. The divisions of pitch are (1) *common* or *natural,* (2) *low,* and (3) *high.*

NOTE.—Strictly speaking the divisions of *pitch* are unlimited, there being as many as the compass of the voice will admit.

5. *Common or natural pitch* is the tone of voice used in conversation, ordinary description and narration.

6. *Low pitch* is any tone of voice lower than the *common* and is used in expressions of sorrow, devotion, awe, despair, and in all solemn or deep emotions.

7. *High pitch* is any tone of voice higher than the *common,* and is used in expressions of excessive joy or grief, sudden fear, and in commanding or calling.

.

QUESTIONS.

1. What does expression include?
2. Define modulation.
3. What is pitch?
4. Name the divisions of pitch.
5. What is common or natural pitch?
6. What is low pitch?
7. What is high pitch?

EXERCISES ON PITCH.

Read each of the following sentences on as low a key as possible with distictness of *articulation* then repeat it successively, gradually elevating the voice until its full compass has been reached, then reverse the process gradually lowering the voice until articulation is indistinct. The student will find this a valuable exercise to strengthen the voice, improve its quality and bring it under perfect control.

1. Give to the winds thy fears.
2. Learn to labor and to wait.—*Longfellow.*
3. Men are led by trifles.—*Napoleon.*
4. Hurrah! for the red, white and blue.
5. Millions for defense but not one cent for tribute. —*Pinckney.*
6. The young are slaves to novelty; the old to custom.
7. 'Tis midnight's holy hour, and silence now
   Is brooding, like a gentle spirit, o'er
   The still and pulseless world.
8. Clarence is come—false, fleeting, perjured Clarence. Seize on him, ye furies, take him to your torments.

NOTE.---Judgment and taste, founded on sentiment and circumstances, must determine the degree of pitch to be used.

LESSON VI.

MODULATION, *Continued.*

1. Rate has reference to the time of utterance in reading and speaking.

2. The divisions of *rate* are (1) *slow*, (2) *medium*, and (3) *rapid.*

3. *Slow rate* is that used in expressions of solemnity, devotion, horror, pathos, and unanimated thought.

4. *Medium rate* is that used in common conversation, narration or description.

5. *Rapid rate* is that used in expressions of joy, anger, excitement and haste.

QUESTIONS.

1. What is rate ?
2. Name the divisions of rate.
3. What is slow rate ?
4. What is medium rate ?
5. What is rapid rate ?

EXERCISES ON RATE.

Read each of the following sentences as slowly as possible without drawling, then repeat it successively, gradually increasing the rate until articulation is indistinct, then reverse the process repeating it slower at each reading. This exercise will enable the student to increase or diminish the rate at pleasure, which is a very important element in reading or speaking.

1. The study of natural history expands and elevates the mind.

2. Every human being has the idea of duty; and to unfold this idea, is the end for which life was given him.

3. One may be wise, though he be poor.

4. Then there was mounting in hot haste ; the steed,
   The mustering squadron, and the clattering car
   Went pouring forward with impetuous speed,
   And swiftly forming in the ranks of war.

5. O, that I had the wings of a dove, that I might fly away and be at rest !

NOTE.---Rate must vary with the nature of the thought to be expressed. It should neither be too slow nor too fast, but the latter is the greater fault and more liable to be made. Mandeville says "Of good elocution, distinct articulation is a fundamental requisite ; and this, in connection with rapid delivery is very rare. The slow speaker may articulate badly; but it has seldom been my good fortune to hear a rapid speaker who articulated well. A slow delivery in general, is, I conceive, absolutely necessary to enable a reader or speaker to comply with the demands of sentiment and emotion."

LESSON VII.

MODULATION, *Continued.*

1. Quality refers to the kind of tone.

2. There are as many qualities of tone as there are kinds of emotion. Eight classes are given : (1) *Pure,* (2) *aspirated,* (3) *orotund,* (4) *guttural,* (5) *nasal,* (6) *falsetto,* (7) *pectoral,* (8) *trembling.*

3. *Pure quality* is that used in common conversation, narration and description.

4. *Orotund* is pure tone deepened and enlarged, and is used in expressions of energy, delight, adoration, and all varieties of sublime emotions.

5. *Guttural* is that in which the voice seems to be produced in the throat, and is used in expressions of hatred, loathing and ill-humor.

6. *Aspirated* is the whisper, or the whisper partly vocalized, and is used in expressions of fear, horror, terror, secrecy and revenge.

7. *Nasal* is that in which the voice seems to pass through the nose.

8. *Falsetto* is any tone above the natural compass of the voice.

9. *Pectoral* is any tone below the natural compass of the voice.

10. *Trembling tone* is that used in excessive grief or pity or to represent enfeebled age.

QUESTIONS.

1. Define quality.
2. How is quality divided?
3. What is pure tone?
4. What is aspirated tone?
5. What is orotund tone?
6. What is falsetto tone?
7. What is guttural tone?
8. What is nasal tone?
9. What is pectoral tone?
10. What is trembling tone?

NOTE.---Sounds may differ as essentially in *quality* as in *pitch*. The organ and violin may accord in pitch yet it is easy to discover the difference in the quality of the tone. Though some voices are more melodious than others, yet all may be improved by proper discipline.

EXERCISES IN QUALITY.

Pure Tone.   NIGHT.

How beautiful is night?
A dewy freshness fills the silent air;
No mist obscures, nor cloud, nor speck, nor stain
    Breaks the serene of heaven;
In full-orbed glory, yonder moon divine
Rolls through the dark-blue depths.
    Beneath her steady ray
The desert-circle spreads
Like the round ocean girded with the sky.
How beautiful is night.—*Southey*

Aspirated.   AMBITION.

How like a mounting devil in the heart
Rules the unrein'd *ambition*! Let it once
But play the monarch, and its haughty brow
Glows with a beauty that bewilders thought
And unthrones peace forever.   Putting on
The very pomp of Lucifer, it turns
The heart to ashes, and with not a spring
Left in the bosom for the spirit's lip,
We look upon our splendor and forget
The thirst of which we perish!—*N. P. Willis.*

Orotund.   TRUE ELOQUENCE.

True eloquence does not consist in speech.   It can
not be brought from afar.   Labor and learning may toil
for it, but they will toil in vain.   Words and phrases may
be marshaled in every way, but they can not compass it.
It must exist in the man, in the subject, and in the occa-

sion.   Affected passion, intense expression, the pomp of declamation, all may aspire after it—they can not reach it.   It comes, if it comes at all, like the out-breaking of a fountain from the earth, or the bursting forth of volcanic fires, with spontaneous, original, native force.—*Webster.*

Guttural.   DEFIANCE.

I loathe you with my bosom ! I scorn you with mine eyes!
And I'll taunt you with my latest breath, and fight you
    till I die.
I ne'er will ask for quarter, and I ne'er will be your slave,
But I'll swim the sea of slaughter till I sink beneath the
    wave.—*The Seminole's Reply.*

Nasal.

             The birds can fly,
             An' why can't I ?
             Must we give in,
             Says he, with a grin,
             That the blue bird an' phoebe
             Are smarter 'n we be ?
             Jest fold our hands, an' see the swaller
             An' blackbird, an' catbird beat us holler ?
                              —*Trowbridge.*

Falsetto.

MRS. CAUDLE URGING THE NEED OF SPRING CLOTHING.

If there's anything in the world I hate, and you know it, it is asking you for money.   I am sure, for myself, I'd rather go without a thing a thousand times—and I do, the more shame for you to let me !

"What do I want now ?" as if you didn't know ! I'm sure

if I'd any money of my own I'd never ask you for a farthing, never! It's painful to me, gracious knows.

What do you say? "If it's painful why so often do it?" I suppose you call that a joke—one of your club-jokes. As I say, I only wish I'd any money of my own. If there is anything that humbles a poor woman it is coming to a man's pocket for every farthing. It's dreadful!

Now Caudle, you hear me, for it isn't often I speak. Pray do you know what month it is! And did you see how the children looked at church to-day?—like nobody else's children!

"What was the matter with them?" Oh, Caudle! how can you ask? Weren't they all in their thick merinoes and beaver bonnets?

What do you say? "What of it?" What! You'll tell me that you didn't see how the Briggs girls in their new chips turned their noses up at 'em? And you didn't see how the Browns looked at the Smiths, and then at our poor girls, as much as to say, "Poor creatures! what figures for the first of May."—*Jerrold.*

Pectoral.   WE WATCHED HER BREATHING.

We watched her breathing through the night,
   Her breathing soft and low,
As in her breast the wave of life
   Kept heaving to and fro.

So silently we seemed to speak,
   So slowly moved about,
As we had lent her half our powers
   To eke her living out.

Our very hopes belied our fears,
  Our fears our hopes belied—
We thought her dying when she slept,
  And sleeping when she died.

For when the morn came dim and sad,
  And chill with early showers,
Her quiet eyelids closed—she had
  She had another morn than ours.—*Hood.*

LESSON VIII.

MODULATION, *Continued.*

1. *Quantity* or *force* refers to the volume of sound without change of *pitch.*

2. Quantity is divided into (1) *subdued,* (2) *moderate,* and (3) *Strong.*

3. *Subdued quantity* is a degree of force less than the common energy of the voice, and is used in expressions of grief, tenderness, caution, admiration, languor and feebleness.

4. *Moderate quantity* is the degree of force usually employed, and is used in expressions of reverence, devotion, narration, description and conversation.

5. *Strong quantity* is a degree of force greater than the common energy of the voice, and is used in expressions of anger, alarm, calling, courage and oratory.

QUESTIONS.

. 1. What is quantity?
2. How is quantity divided?
3. What is subdued quantity?
4. What is moderate quantity?
5. What is strong quantity?

EXERCISES IN QUANTITY.

Subdued quantity.   CURFEW.

Solemnly, mournfully,
   Dealing its dole,
The Curfew bell
   Is beginning to toll.

Cover the embers,
   And put out the light ;
Toil comes with the morning,
   And rest with the night.

Dark grows the windows,
   And quenched is the fire ;
Sound fades into silence,—
   All footsteps retire.

No voice in the chamber,
   No sound in the hall!
Sleep and oblivion
   Reign over all !—*Longfellow.*

Moderate quantity.   LINCOLN'S DEATH.

The nation rises up at every stage of his coming ;
cities and states are as pall-bearers, and the cannon beats

the hours in solemn progression ; dead, dead, dead, he yet speaketh.

Is Washington dead? Is Hampden dead? Is David dead? Is any man that ever was fit to live dead? * *

* Disenthralled from the flesh, and risen to the unobstructed sphere where passion never comes, he begins his illimitable work.

His life is now grafted upon the Infinite, and will be fruitful as no earthly life can be. Pass on. Four years ago, oh Illinois, we took from your midst an untried man from among the people. * * * Behold, we return him to you a mighty conquerer, not thine any more, but the nation's ; not ours, but the world's. Give him place, oh ye prairies ! In the midst of this great continent his dust shall rest, a sacred treasure to myriads who shall pilgrim to that shrine to kindle anew their patriotism. Ye winds, that move over the mighty spaces of the west, chant his requiem ! Ye people, behold the martyr, whose drops of blood, as so many articulate words, plead for fidelity, for law, for liberty.—*Beecher.*

Strong quantity. THE LIFE BOAT.

Quick ! Man the life-boat ! See yon bark
    That drives before the blast !
There's a rock ahead, the fog is dark,
And the storm comes thick and fast.
Can human power, in such an hour,
    Avert the doom that's o'er her ?
Her main-mast's gone, but she still drives on
To the fatal reef before her.
    The life-boat ! Man the life-boat.

LESSON IX.

MODULATION, *Continued.*

1. *Stress* has reference to the manner of applying emphasis to one or more words of a sentence.

2. Stress is divided into (1) *initial* or *radical*, (2) *final*, (3) *sustained*, (4) *mediau* or *swell*, (5) *compound*, and (6) *intermittent* or *tremulous.*

3. *Initial* or *radical stress* is that in which the emphasis falls upon the beginning of a word or phrase, and gradually diminishes.

4. *Final stress* is that in which the emphasis is gradually increased.

5. *Sustained stress* is that in which the emphasis commences, continues and ends with the same force.

6. *Median* or *swell stress* is that in which the emphasis is applied with the greatest force in the middle of the sound.

7. *Compound stress* is that in which the emphasis is applied with the greatest force at the initial and final parts of the sound.

8. *Intermittent* or *tremulous stress* is that in which the emphasis is applied in wave-like impulses.

QUESTIONS.

1. What is stress ?
2. How is stress divided ?
3. Define initial stress.
4. Define final stress.
5. Define sustained stress.
6. What is median stress ?
7. What is compound stress ?
8. Define intermittent stress.

EXERCISES IN STRESS.

Initial stress.　　˙THE LAW OF THE LORD.

The law of the Lord is perfect, converting the soul;
The testimony of the Lord is sure, making wise the simple.
The statutes of the Lord are right, rejoicing the heart ;
The commandent of the Lord is pure, enlightening the
　　eyes.
The fear of the Lord is clean, enduring forever ;
The judgments of the Lord are true and righteous alto-
　　gether.

More to be desired are they than gold, yea, than much
fine gold ; sweeter also than honey and the honeycomb.
Moreover by them is thy servant warned ; and in keeping of them there is great reward.—*Bible.*

Final stress.　　　　MOUNTAINS.

Mountains ! who was your Builder ? Who laid your
awful foundations in the central fires, and piled your rocks
and snow-capped summits among the clouds ? Who
placed you in the gardens of the world, like noble altars
on which to offer the sacrificial gifts of many nations ?
Who reared your rocky walls in the barren desert, like
towering pyramids, like monumental mounds, like giants'
graves, like dismantled piles of royal ruins, telling a
mournful tale of glory, once bright, but now fled forever,
as flee the dreams of a midsummer's night ? Who gave
you a home in the islands of the sea—those emeralds that
gleam among the waves—those stars of ocean that mock
the beauty of the stars of night ?

Mountains ! I know who built you. It was God ! His
name is written on your foreheads. He laid your corner-
stones on that glorious morning when the orchestra of

heaven sounded the anthem of creation. He clothed your high, imperial forms in royal robes. He gave you a snowy garment, and wove for you a cloudy veil of crimson and gold. He crowned you with a diadem of icy jewels ; pearls from the arctic seas ; gems from the frozen pole.—*Morse*.

Sustained stress.   STUDIES.

Studies serve for delight, for ornament, and for ability. Their chief use for delight is in privateness and retiring ; for ornament, is in discourse ; and for ability, is in the judgment and disposition of business. For expert men can execute, and perhaps, judge of particulars, one by one ; but the general counsels, and the plots and marshaling of affairs, come best from those that are learned. —*Bacon*.

Median stress.   EXTRACT FROM THE BURIAL OF MOSES.

> By Nebo's lonely mountain,
> On this side Jordan's wave,
> In a vale in the land of Moab,
> There lies a lonely grave ;
> But no man dug that sepulchre,
> And no man saw it e'er,
> For the angels of God upturned the sod
> And laid the dead man there.—*Alexander*.

Compound stress.   CATALINE'S DEFENSE.

Banished from *Rome* ? What's *banished*, but set *free*
From daily contact of the things I *loathe ?*
"Tried and convicted *traitor ? Who* says this ?
Who'll *prove* it, at his *peril*, on *my* head ?
Banished ! I *thank* you for it. It breaks my chain.
I held some slack *allegiance* till *this* hour ;

But *uow* my sword's my *own.*   Smile on my Lords ;
I *scorn* to count what *feelings*, withered *hopes*,
Strong *provocations*, bitter, burning *wrongs*,
I have within my heart's hot cells shut up,
To *leave* you in your *lazy dignities.*
But here I stand and *scoff* you ; here I fling
Hatred and full *defiance* in your face.
Your consul's *merciful !* For this all *thanks !"—Croly.*

Intermittent stress.   FROM BINGEN ON THE RHINE.

His voice grew faint and hoarser—his grasp was childish
    weak—
His eyes put on a dying look—he sighed and ceased to
    speak ;
His comrade bent to lift him, but the spark of life had fled—
The soldier of the Legion, in a foreign land was dead !
And the soft moon rose up slowly, and calmly she looked
    down
On the red sand of the battlefield, with bloody corpses
    strown ;
Yea, calmly on that dreadful scene her pale light seemed
    to shine,
As it shone on distant Bingen—fair Bingen on the Rhine !
                                            —Mrs. Norton.

LESSON X.

MODULATION, *Continued.*

1. *Inflection* is the change of pitch used in reading
and speaking.

2 There are but two inflections; the *rising* and the
falling.   For convenience these are divided into *simple
rising, compound rising, simple falling,* and *compound
falling.*

3.   The *simple rising inflection* is that in which the voice glides upward and suggests incomplete sense.

4.   The *compound rising inflection* is·that in which the voice begins with the downward and ends with the upward slide.

5.   The *simple falling inflection* is that in which the voice glides downward and suggests complete sense.

6.   The *compound falling inflection* is that in which the voice begins with the upward and ends with the downward slide.

7.   *Monotone* is a sameness of tone or absence of inflection, and is properly used in sublime or solemn expressions.

8.   *Cadence* is the fall of the voice at the end of a sentence.

QUESTIONS.

1.   What is inflection ?
2.   How many inflections are there ?
3.   What is the simple rising inflection ?
4.   What is the compound rising inflection ?
5.   What is the simple falling inflection ?
6.   What is the compound falling inflection ?
7.   Define monotone.
8.   Define cadence.

RULES FOR THE USE OF INFLECTIONS.

1.   Direct questions usually require the rising inflection, and their answers the falling.

EXAMPLES.

1. Will you accept my offer ? I will.
2. Is your brother well ? Yes.
3. Will you leave us ? No.

NOTE.—Direct questions repeated with emphasis, or used in earnest appeal, take the falling inflection.

2. Indirect questions and their answers usually require the falling inflection.

EXAMPLES.

1. How long must I wait ? Until to-morrow.
2. How many came with you ? Ten.
3. Who said, "Millions for defense but not a cent for tribute ?" Pinckney.

NOTE.—Indirect questions repeated, or used with emphasis take the rising inflection.

3. Contrasted words or expressions require opposite inflections.

EXAMPLES.

1. A wise son maketh a glad father ; but a foolish son is the heaviness of his mother.
2. Sink or swim, live or die, survive or perish, I give my hand and heart to this vote.

NOTE.—Of words contrasted the one which has the greater emphasis takes the falling inflection, and the one which expresses negation the rising inflection.

4. Expressions of anger, authority, reproach, and all others uttered with emphasis usually require the falling inflection.

EXAMPLES.

1. Silence thou slave, thou coward, away from my sight.
2. Charge, Chester, charge ! on Stanley, on !
3. Go to the ant, thou sluggard, consider *her* ways, and be *wise*.

5.   Expressions of grief, emotion and kindness usually require the rising inflection.

EXAMPLES.

1. O my son Absalom ! my son, my son, Absalom !
2. He bleeds ! he falls ! his death-bed is the field !
His dirge the trumpet, and his bier the shield !

6.   The compound inflections are used in expressions of irony, derision, sarcasm and contrast.

EXAMPLES.

1. *You* do not know him, as *we* do.
2. He is a *fine* specimen of humanity.
3. One may be *wise*, though he be *poor*.

LESSON XI.

EMPHASIS

1.   Emphasis is a special stress of voice on one or more words of a sentence.

NOTE.—There are three ways of indicating emphasis. (1) by *italics*, (2) by small CAPITALS, and (3) by large CAPITALS.

2.   Emphasis is divided into (1) *absolute*, (2) *antithetic*, or *relative*, and (3) *cumulative*.

3.   *Absolute emphasis* is that which is used upon words not compared with others in the sentence.

4.   *Antithetic* or *relative emphasis* is that which is used upon words contrasted with others in the sentence.

5.   *Cumulative emphasis* is that which is used upon a succession of words.

1.   What is emphasis ?
2.   How is emphasis divided ?
3.   What is absolute emphasis ?
4.   What is antithetic emphasis ?
5.   What is cumulative emphasis ?

NOTE.—Emphasis has the same relation to the words of a sentence that accent has to the syllables of a word.

"By the proper use of emphasis, we are enabled to impart animation and interest to conversation and reading. Its importance can not be over estimated, as the meaning of a sentence often depends upon the proper placing of the emphasis. If readers have a desire to produce an impression on hearers, and read what they *understand* and *feel*, they will generally place emphasis on the right words."—*Watson.*

RULES FOR THE USE OF EMPHASIS.

1.   All words and phrases, to which special attention is directed, are emphasized.

EXAMPLES.

1.   Life is *real !* Life is *earnest !*
2.   The *sun* rises in the east.
3.   If you are *men* follow me.

2.   All words and phrases contrasted are emphasized.

EXAMPLES.

1.   *Wit* laughs *at* things ; *humor* laughs *with* them.
2.   *Clay* was the greater *orator* ; *Webster*, the greater *statesman.*
3.   *Just men* only are *free* ; the rest are *slaves.*

3.   Important words or phrases repeated, generally require an increase of emphasis.

EXAMPLES.

1. His *sorrow*, his ANGUISH, his DEATH were caused by your carelessness.
2. I *never* would lay down my arms—*never!* NEVER! NEVER!
3. "We must *fight*, sir ; I repeat it, we must FIGHT.

TO THE TEACHER.—Use miscellaneous selections to test the pupils' knowledge of the rules of emphasis, having them name the words emphasized, and the kind of emphasis used.

LESSON XII.

PERSONATION.

1. *Personation* is the variation of the voice used to represent two or more persons as speaking, and is employed in reading dialogues and selections of a conversational nature.

EXAMPLES FOR PARCTICE.

One of the People.—We'll hear the will : read it, Mark Antony.

All.—The will! the will! we will hear Cæsar's will.

Antony.—Have patience, gentle friends, I must not read it. It is not meet you know how Cæsar loved you.   *   *   *   *   *   *   *   *

People.—Read the will ; we will hear it, Antony.

Antony.—Will you be patient? Will you wait awhile ?

All.—The will! the testament !

Antony.—You will compel me then to read the will? Then make a ring about the corpse of Cæsar, and let me

show you him that made the will. If you have tears,
prepare to shed them now.

First Citizen.—O piteous spectacle !

Second Gitizen.—O noble Cæsar !

Third Citizen.—We will be revenged ! Revenge !
about—seek—burn—fire—kill—slay ! let not a traitor
live.

Antony.—Stay, countrymen.

First Citizen.—Peace there ; hear the noble Antony.

Second Citizen.—We'll hear him, we'll follow him, we'll
die with him.—*Shakespeare.*

TO THE TEACHER.—Take additional exercises from
SELECTIONS IN READING for drill in personation ; it will
be found a valuable means of securing control of the voice.
Concert exercises in personation will assist in awakening
an interest in the work, as well as in disciplining the
voices of the class.

2. *Transition* is a variation in the manner of delivery,
to represent change of sentiment or meaning.

3. *Slur* is a smooth gliding movement of the voice
heard in reading and speaking, and is used in cases of
antithesis, explanation, repetition, and in parenthetical
clauses.

QUESTIONS.

1. What is personation ?

2. What is transition ?

3. What is slur ?

LESSON XIII.

PAUSES.

1. *Pauses* are the cessations of voice in reading or
speaking, used to add force to the expression, also to mark
grammatical construction.

2. *Punctuation* is the art of separating written or printed composition into sentences and parts of sentences by marks or points. "Its primary object is to bring out the writer's meaning, and so far only is it an aid to the reader."—*Quackenbos.*

3. Pauses are of two kinds, (1) *grammatical* and (2) *rhetorical.*

4. *Grammatical pauses* are those used to indicate the nature or meaning of the sentence.

5. *Rhetorical pauses* are those used to add force to the expression, where the construction does not admit of a grammatical pause.

6. The grammatical pauses are *comma*, (,) *semicolon*,(;) *colon*, (:) *period*, (.) *interrogation*, (?) and *exclamation*. (!)

7. The *rhetorical* pause is usually represented by the dash. (—)

QUESTIONS.

1. What are pauses?
2. What is punctuation?
3. Pauses are of how many kinds? Name them.
4. What are grammatical pauses?
5. What are rhetorical pauses?
6. Name the grammatical pauses?
7. How is the rhetorical pause represented?

RULES FOR THE USE OF PAUSES.

1. *Comma :* The comma is employed in separating words, phrases and clauses which make imperfect sense, but are closely connected with the rest of the sentence.

2. *Semicolon :* The semicolon is employed in separating the members of sentences which make perfect sense, and which are united by connectives expressed.

3. *Colon :* The colon is employed in separating the members of sentences which make perfect sense, and which are united by connectives understood.

4, *Period :* The period is placed at the end of every declarative and imperative sentence, and after every abbreviated word.

5. *Interrogation :* The interrogation point is placed after ever interrogative sentence or clause.

6. *Exclamation :* The exclamation point is placed after every exclamatory sentence or clause, and interjection.

7. *Dash :* The dash is used before exclamatory words repeated, before a change in the construction of the sense, after a member abruptly broken off, and after a sentence which ends abruptly. Also to show the omission of letters or figures.

LESSON XIV.

GESTURE.

1. *Gesture* is action or attitude used to express or enforce sentiment and emotion.

2. *Gesture* includes (1) *attitude*, (2) *gesticulation*, and (3) *facial expression.*

3. *Attitude* is the position of the body when at rest in expressing or enforcing sentiment or emotion.

4. *Gesticulation* is the movement of the body, or change of position, in expressing or enforcing sentiment or emotion.

5. *Facial expression* is the language of the countenance with reference to feeling or emotion.

6.   *Attitude* is usually classified as (1) *firm*, (2) *relax*, (3) *advancing*, and (4) *receding*.

7.   A *firm attitude* is when the muscles are firm and rigid, and is suited to expressions of courage, sublimity and pride.

8.   A *relax attitude* is when the muscles are relax and loose, and is suited to expressions of fatigue, great fear and unemotional language.

9.   An *advancing attitude* is when the body is inclined forward, and is suited to expressions of caution, devotion, welcome, listening, etc.

10.   A *receding attitude* is when the body is inclined backward, and is suited to expressions of abhorence, defiance, disdain. etc.

QUESTIONS.

1.   What is gesture?
2.   What does gesture include?
3.   Define attitude.
4.   What is gesticulation?
5.   What is facial expression?
6.   How is attitude classified?
7.   What is meant by a firm attitude?
8.   Define relax attitude.
9.   What is an advancing attitude?
10.   What is a receding attitude?

LESSON XV.

GESTURE, *Continued*.

1.   *Gesticulation* includes movements of the (1) head, (2) upper limbs, and (3) lower limbs.

2. The positions of the head are (1) erect, (2) inclined backward, (3) inclined forward, and (4) inclined to one side.

3. An erect position of the head indicates confidence, firmness, dignity, manliness, honor, courage, etc.

4. Head inclined backward indicates mirth, pride, etc.

5. Head inclined forward indicates shame, humility, grief, reflection, etc.

6. Head inclined to one side indicates carelessness, indifference, feebleness, etc.

7. The movements of the upper limbs include those of the (1) hands and (2) arms.

8. The positions of the hand with reference to the palm, are known as (1) prone, (2) supine, (3) vertical, and (4) repelling. With reference to the fingers as (1) natural, (2) vertical, (3) indexical, (4) clenched, (5) extended, and (6) clasped.

9. The *prone* position of the hand is the palm downward, and is suited to expressions of secrecy, concealment, etc.

10. The *supine* position is the palm upward, and is suited to expressions of information, advice, etc.

11. The *vertical* position is the palm perpendicular, and is suited to expressions of solemn obligation, amazement, etc.

12. The *repelling* position is the palm outward, and is suited to expressions of repulsion, dislike, etc.

13. The *natural* position of the fingers is when they hang loosely, and is suited to ordinary conversation or discourse.

14. The *vertical* position is the fingers pointing upward, and is suited to appeals to duty, surprise, etc.

15. The *indexical* position is the forefinger extended, and is used in pointing.

16. The *clenched* position is the hand closed tightly, and is suited to expressions of violence, anger, etc.

17. The *clasped* position is the hands united and closed, and is used in earnest entreaty and supplication.

QUESTIONS.

1. What does gesticulation include?
2. Name the positions of the head.
3. What does the erect position indicate?
4. What does the head inclined backward indicate?
5. What does the head inclined forward indicate?
6. What does the head inclined to one side indicate?
7. What do the movements of the upper limbs indicate?
8. Name the positions of the hand?
9. Define the prone position.
10. Define the supine position.
11. Define the vertical position.
12. Define the repelling position.
13. What is meant by the natural position of the fingers?
14. What is meant by the vertical position of the fingers?
15. What is the indexical position?
16. What is the clenched position?
17. What is the clasped position of the hands?

LESSON XVI.

GESTURE, *Continued.*

1. The positions of the arm are (1) front, (2) lateral, (3) oblique, and (4) backward.

2. The *front* position is the arm directly in front or before the person, and is used in emphatic assertion or direct appeal.

3. The *lateral* position is the arm extended to the right or left, and is used in language of a general nature, and appeals to the intellect.

4. The *oblique* position is the arm between the front and lateral positions.

5. The *backward* or *back oblique* position is the arm back of the lateral position.

6. The positions of the lower limbs are (1) advanced, (2) retired, and (3) lateral.

7. The *advanced* position is the movement of either foot forward.

8. The *retired* position is the movement of either foot backward. —

9. The *lateral* position is the movement of either foot to the right or left of first position.

10. *Facial* expression is named as (1) natural, (2) smiling, (3) averted, (4) dejected, (5) staring, etc,

11. The *natural* expression indicates satisfaction, reverence, etc.

12. The *smiling* expression indicates cheerfulness, good will, etc.

13. The *averted* expression indicates perplexity, disgust, etc.

14. The *dejected* expression indicates shame, sorrow, humility, etc.

15. The *staring* expression indicates boasting, defiance, etc.

QUESTIONS.

1. Name the positions of the arms.
2. What is the front position ?
3. What is the lateral position ?

4.   What is the oblique position ?
5.   What is the backward position ?
6.   Name the positions of the lower limbs.
7.   What is the advanced position ?
8.   What is the retired position ?
9.   What is the lateral position ?
10. Name some of the facial expressions.
11. What does the natural expression of the face
     indicate ?
12. What does the smiling expression of the face
     indicate ;
13. What does the averted expression of the face
     indicate ?
14. What does the dejected expression of the face
     indicate ?
15. What does the staring expression of the face
     indicate ?

TO THE TEACHER.—The following excellent advice
upon gesture, is from Cole's Institute Reader :

"Do not attempt too much in gesture, but what you do
teach, teach thoroughly.   The great object to be aimed
at is gracefulness."   *   *   *   "The key to a graceful
and easy manner is self possession ; you can not more
easily cultivate this than by class drills in movements."
*   *   *   "Stand in front of the class, speak the words
around, *beneath*, *on high* ; and on pronouncing each word
make the appropriate gesture.   Use the hand and arm
without pronouncing the words.   Teacher count and the
class execute the movements together."   *   *   *   "The
art of graceful gesticulation lies in keeping the muscles
moderately relaxed."   *   *   *   "As a rule, oratorical
gesture should be executed in easy, graceful curves ; in-
vectives, in straight lines and angles.   The movements
of the feet, as well as those of the hands, must be looked

after.   While too much stepping in declamation is objectionable, as giving the appearance of rant, too little, on the other hand, conveys the impression of stiffness."

The posture should be erect but not stiff.

"He who in earnest studies o'er his part,
Will find true nature cling about his heart.
The modes of grief are not included all
In the white handkerchief and mournful drawl ;
A single look more marks the internal woe,
Than all the windings of the lengthened Oh !
Up to the face the quick sensation flies,
And darts its meaning from the speaking eyes.
Love, transport, madness, anger, scorn, despair,
And all the passions, all the soul is there."—*Lloyd*.

TO THE TEACHER.

I. METHODS.

There are five methods of teaching reading, viz :   Alphabetical, phonic, word, sentence and combined.

1.   The alphabetical method is that in which the names and forms of the letters are first taught, then to arrange them into words and sentences.

2.   The phonic method is that in which the elementary sounds are taught by the analysis of simple words, and the use of diacritical marks.

3.   The word method is that in which the words are first taught to represent ideas, by first presenting objects, pictures, etc., and then the words which name them.

4.   The sentence method is that in which whole sentences are first taught to represent some thought, by first presenting the thought and then the sentence representing it.

5. The combined method is that in which simple words are first taught, and then the letters and sounds which compose them.

II. PRIMARY READING.

The teacher should have a well defined plan of what is to be accomplished, and a distinct and vivid conception of how to execute that plan in all branches of school work, and especially is this true in teaching reading. The leading objects to be obtained in primary reading are (1) ability to name words at sight, (2) a correct articulation, and (3) ability to read intelligently, and with correct expression. These must be attended to in each lesson if success is desired.

A few hints to the primary teacher may not be amiss.

1. Be in earnest. "Earnestness is the charm, the magnetism of the school room."

2. Have the pupil stand, and stand erect, while reading. If the class stand, the reader should advance a step to the front. This requires unwearied patience and persevering effort.

3. The book should be held in the left hand, sufficiently high to enable the pupil to stand erect, with chin well up.

4. Avoid assigning too long lessons.

5. Each syllable and word should be pronounced distinctly.

6. Secure and hold the attention of the entire class during the recitation.

7. Ask questions upon the lesson read, to cultivate the memory, and to stimulate inquiry.

8. Teach your pupils to write script as well as to print. The change from one to the other will add interest and pleasure to their work. In each insist upon neatness of execution.

9. Call upon pupils promiscuously. Change the order of conducting a recitation occasionally, having pupils read in concert, read from pause to pause, etc.

10. Remember that the time of recitation belongs to the class and not to the school.

III. INTERMEDIATE READING.

Many of the hints under primary reading are as applicable here as there, and should be carefully studied. The objects to be attained in intermediate reading, are (1) to assist pupils in enlarging their vocabulary, (2) to teach proper vocal expressions, and (3) to teach how to study. We add a few hints to the intermediate teacher.

1. Prepare for each recitation by a careful study of the lesson before hearing it recited.

2. In assigning lessons, point out the special points to be studied—*teach how to study.*

3. Require pupils to select lists of words from the reading lesson and to indicate the sounds of the letters by diacritical marks.

4. Teach pupils how to use the dictionary, and to ascertain the meaning of the words found in each lesson.

5. Have frequent exercises in writing sentences which shall contain certain words found in each lesson.

6. In reading verse care should be taken to read with reference to the sense and not to the rhythm.

7. Allow pupils to make short selections occasionally, from readers or other sources, to awaken an interest in the work.

8. Give occasional half days to exercises in select readings and declamations.

9. In teaching gestures, as in all else, let your motto be, *not how much, but how well.*

10. Teach the use of capital letters and marks of punctuation as they occur in the lessons.

IV. ADVANCED READING.

The rules already given contain much that is of practical value, and should be carefully studied before taking up the advanced lessons. The objects to be attained in advanced reading, are (1) the pronunciation of new and difficult words, (2) the analysis and study of words, (3) the analysis and critical study of a reading exercise, and (4) the teaching of some fact in elocution.

We annex a few hints.

1. Constant use of the dictionary should be made to ascertain the meaning and pronunciation of new and difficult words. Make lists of words frequently mispronounced or badly articulated for special drill.

2. Give much time to practice in articulation, emphasis, inflection, etc.

3. Aanalyze words both by syllable and by sound.

4. Call upon pupils occasionally to read lessons without special preparation.

5. Teach pupils to look off from their books occasionally as they read. It will enable them to give better expression to the sentiment, and will be more pleasing to those who listen.

6. Number your class, and occasionally call by number, having them read until the next number is called.

7. Divide the class in sections, twos, threes or fours, and have them read by sections.

8. See that the pupil stands erect, speaks deliberately, and articulates distinctly.

A STORY OF SCHOOL.

The red light shone through the open door, .
From round the declining sun ;
And fantastic shadows, all about
. On the dusty floor were thrown,
As the factory clock told the hour of five,
. And the school was almost done.

The mingled hum of the busy town,
  Rose faint from her lower plain ;
And we saw the steeple over the trees,
  With its motionless golden vane ;
And heard the cattle's musical low,
  And the rustle of standing grain.

In the open casement a lingering bee
  Murmured a drowsy tune ;
And, from the upland meadows, a song
  In the lull of the afternoon
Had come, on the air that wandered by,
  Ladened with the scents of June.

Our tasks were finished and lessons said,
  And we sat all hushed and still,
Listening to catch the purl of the brook,
  And the whir of the distant mill,
And waited the word of dismissal, that yet
  Waited the master's will.

The master was old and his form was bent,
    And scattered and white his hair ;
But his heart was young, and there ever dwelt
    A calm and kindly air,
Like the halo over a pictured saint,
    On his face, marked deep with care.

His eyes were closed and his wrinkled hands
    Were folded over his vest,
As wearily back in his old arm-chair
    He reclined as if to rest ;
And the golden streaming sunlight fell
    On his brow, and down his breast.

We waited in reverent silence long,
    And silence the master kept ;
Though still the accustomed saintly smile
    Over his features crept ;
And we thought, worn with the lengthened toil
    Of the summer's day, he slept.

So we quietly rose and left our seats,
    And outward into the sun,
From the gathering shades of the dusty room,
    Stole silently, one by one.
For we knew, by the distant striking clock,
    It was time the school was done.

And left the master, sleeping alone,
    Alone in his high-backed chair,
With his eyelids closed, and his withered palms
    Folded as if in prayer ;
And the mingled light and smile on his face,
    And we knew not that DEATH was there.
                            —*William R. Hart.*

THE DEATH OF HAMILTON.

"How are the mighty fallen !" And, regardless as we are of vulgar deaths, shall not the fall of the mighty affect us ? A short time since, and he, who is the occasion of our sorrow, was the ornament of his country. He stood on an eminence, and glory covered him. From that eminence he has fallen ; suddenly, forever, fallen. His intercourse with the living world is now ended, and those who would hereafter find him, must seek him in the grave. There, cold and lifeless, is the heart which just now was the seat of friendship ; there, dim and sightless is the eye, whose radiant and enlivening orb beamed with intelligence ; and there, closed forever, are those lips, on whose persuasive accents we have so often, and so lately, hung with transport ! From the darkness which rests upon his tomb, there proceeds, methinks, a light in which it is clearly seen, that those gaudy objects, which men pursue, are only phantoms. In this light how dimly shines the splendor of victory ; how humble appears the majesty of grandeur ! The bubble, which seemed to have so much solidity, has burst, and we again see, that all below the sun is vanity.

True, the funeral eulogy has been pronounced, the sad and solemn procession has moved, the badge of mourning has already been decreed, and presently the sculptured marble will lift up its front, proud to perpetuate the name of Hamilton, and rehearse to the passing traveler his virtues ; (just tributes of respect, and to the living useful,) but to him, mouldering in his narrow and humble habitation, what are they ? How vain ! how unavailing !

Approach, and behold, while I lift from his sepulchre its covering ! Ye admirers of his greatness ! Ye emulous

of his talents and his fame, approach and behold him now.
How pale! How silent! No martial bands admire the
adroitness of his movements ; no fascinating throng weep,
and melt, and tremble at his eloquence! Amazing
change! A shroud! A coffin! A narrow, subterraneous
cabin!—this is all that now remains of Hamilton! And
is this all that remains of Hamilton? During a life so
transitory, what lasting monument, then, can our fondest
hopes erect?

My brethren! we stand on the borders of an awful
gulf, which is swallowing up all things human ; and is
there, amidst this universal wreck, nothing stable, nothing abiding, nothing immortal, on which poor, frail, dying
man can fasten? Ask the hero, ask the statesman, whose
wisdom you have been accustomed to revere, and he will
tell you. He will tell you, did I say? He has already
told you, from his death-bed ; and his illumined spirit
still whispers from the heavens, with well-known eloquence, the solemn admonition : "Mortals hastening to
the tomb, and once the companions of my pilgrim-
age, take warning and avoid my errors ; cultivate
the virtues I have recommended ; choose the Savior I
have chosen ; live disinterestedly ; live for immortality ;
and would you rescue any thing from final dissolution, lay
it up in God."

THE MOUNTAIN HYMN.

O *dread* and *silent* Mount! I gaze upon thee,
Till thou, still present to the bodily sense,
Didst vanish from my thought, entranced in prayer,
I worshiped the *Invisible* alone.
Yet like some sweet beguiling melody,

So sweet we know not we are listening to it,
Thou, the meanwhile, wast blending with my thought,
Yea, with my life and life's own secret joy ;
Till the dilating soul, enrapt, transfused,
Into the mighty vision passing,—there,
As in her natural form, swelled vast to heaven !

Awake, my soul ! not only passive praise
Thou owest ; not alone these swelling tears,
Mute thanks and secret ecstacy.   Awake,
Voice of sweet song ! awake, my heart, awake !
Green vales and icy cliffs, all join my hymn.

Thou first and chief, sole sovereign of the vale !
O ! struggling with the darkness all the night,
And visited all night by troops of stars,
Or when they climb the sky, or when they sink !
Companion of the morning star at dawn,
Thyself earth's rosy star, and of the dawn
Co-herald, wake ! O wake ! and utter praise !
Who sank thy sunless pillars deep in earth ?
Who filled thy countenance with rosy light ?
Who made thee parent of perpetual streams ?

And you, ye five wild torrents fiercely glad,
Who called you forth from night and utter death,
From dark and icy caverns called you forth,
Down those precipitous, black, jagged rocks,
Forever shattered, and the same forever ?
Who gave you your invulnerable life,
Your strength, your speed, your fury, and your joy,
Unceasing thunder and eternal foam ?
And who commanded, and the silence came,
"Here let the billows stiffen and have rest ?"

Ye ice-falls ! ye that from the mountain's brow
Adown enormous ravines slope amain—
Torrents, methinks, that heard a mighty voice,
And stopped at once amid their maddest plunge !
Motionless torrents ! Silent cataracts !
Who made you glorious as the gates of heaven
Beneath the keen full moon ? Who bade the sun
Clothe you with rainbows ? Who with living flowers
Of loveliest blue, spread garlands at your feet ?
"GOD !" let the torrents, like a shout of nations,
Answer ; and let the ice-plains echo,—"GOD !"
"GOD !" sing ye meadow-streams with gladsome voice !
Ye pine groves, with your soft and soul-like sounds,
And they, too, have a voice, yon piles of snow,
And in their perilous fall shall thunder,—"GOD !"

Ye living flowers that skirt the eternal frost !
Ye wild goats sporting round the eagle's nest !
Ye eagles, playmates of the mountain storm !
Ye lightnings, the dread arrows of the clouds !
Ye signs and wonders of the elements !
Utter forth "GOD !" and fill the hills with praise !

Thou, too, hoar Mount ! with thy sky-pointing peaks,
Oft from whose brow the avalanche, unheard,
Shoots downward, glittering through the pure serene,
Into the depth of clouds that vail thy breast,
Thou too, again, stupendous Mountain, thou,
That as I raise my head, awhile bowed low
In adoration, upward from thy base,
Slow traveling with dim eyes suffused with tears,
Solemnly seemest, like a vapory cloud,
To rise before me,—rise, O ever rise !
Rise, like a cloud of incense, from the earth !

Thou kingly spirit, throned among the hills,
Thou dread embassador from earth to heaven,
Great Hierarch ! tell thou the silent sky,
And tell the stars, and tell yon rising sun,
"Earth, with her thousand voices, praises GOD."
—*Coleridgc.*

THE SPELLING SCHOOL.

The child-world, in this quarter, is in an active state
of unrest. The school in the Quaker neighborhood has
sent a challenge, in due form, to this district, to spell ; so
to-night the war of words is to be waged in the white
school-house on the hill. There is a great overhauling of
old "Elementaries," and turning over of clean collars,
preparatory to the grand *melee.*

Spelling schools ! Have you forgotten them ? When
from all the regions round about, they gathered into the
old log school-house, with its huge fireplace that yawned
like the main entrance to Avernus. How the sleigh-bells
—the old-fashioned bells, big in the middle of the string,
and growing "small by degrees and beautifully less" to-
ward the broad brass buckle—chimed in every direction
long before night, the gathering of the clans.

There came one school, the Master—give him a capital M, for he is entitled to it—Master and all bundled into
one huge, red, double sleigh, strewn with an abundance
of straw, and tucked up like a Christmas pie, with a half-
score of buffalo robes ; then a half dozen cutters, each
with its young man and maiden, then two more ; and
then, again, a pair of jumpers, mounting a great out-
landish-looking bin, heaped up, pressed down, and run-

ning over, with small collections of humanity, picked up *en route* from a great many homes, and all as merry as kittens in a basket of wool.

And the bright eyes, and ripe, red lips, that one caught a glimpse of beneath those pink-lined, quilted hoods, and the silvery laughs that escaped from the woolen mufflers and fur tippets they wore then—who does not remember? —who can forget them?

The school-house destined to be the arena for the conflict has been swept and garnished; boughs of evergreen adorn the smoke-stained and battered walls. The little pellets of chewed paper have all been swept down from the ceiling, and two pails of water have been brought from the spring and set on the bench in the entry, with the immemorial tincup—a wise provision, for warm work is that spelling.

The big boys have fanned and replenished the fire, till the old chimney fairly jars with the roaring flames, and the sparks fly out of the top like a furnace—the oriflamme of the battle. The two masters are there; the two schools are there; and such a hum, and such a moving to and fro!

The oaken ferule comes down upon the desk with emphasis. What the roll of the drum is to armies, the ruler is to this whispering, laughing young troop. The challenged are ranged on one side of the house; the challengers on the other. Back seats, middle seats, low front seats, all filled. Some of the fathers and grandfathers, who could, no doubt, upon occasion, "shoulder the crutch and show how fields were won," occupy the bench of honor near the desk.

Now for the preliminaries: The reputed best speller on each side chooses. "Susan Brown!" Out comes a round-eyed little creature, blushing like a peony. Who'd have thought it? Such a little thing, and chosen first.

"Moses Jones!" Out comes Moses, an awkward fellow, with a shock of red hair surrounding his broad brow. The girls laugh at him ; but what he doesn't know in the "Elementary" isn't worth knowing.

"Jane Murray!" Out trips Jane, fluttered as a bride, and takes her place next to the caller. She's a pretty girl, but a sorry speller. Don't you hear the whisper round the house ? "Why, that's John's sweetheart." John is the leader, and a battle lost with Jane by his side would be sweeter than a victory won without her.

And so they go on "calling names," until five or six champions stand forth ready to do battle, and the contest is fairly begun. Down goes one after another, as words of three syllables are followed by those of four, and these again by words of similar pronunciation and divers significations, until only Moses and Susan remain.

The spelling book has been exhausted, yet there they stand. Dictionaries are turned over ; memories are ransacked for "words of learned length and thundering sound," until, by and by, Moses comes down like a tree, and Susan flutters there still, like a little leaf aloft, that the frosts and fall have forgotten.

Polysyllables follow polysyllables, and by and by, Susan hesitates just a breath or two, and twenty tongues are working their way through the labyrinth of letters in a twinkling. Little Susan sinks into a chink left for her on the crowded seat, and there is a lull in the battle.

Then they all stand in a solid phalanx by schools, and the struggle is to spell each other down ; and down they go like leaves in wintry weather, and the victory is declared for *our* district and the school is dismissed.

Then comes the hurrying and bundling, the whispering and glancing, the pairing off and the tumbling in. There are hearts that flutter and hearts that ache ; "mit-

tens" that are not worn, secret hopes that are not real-
ized, and fond looks that are not returned.   There is a
jingling of bells at the door ; one after another the sleighs
dash up, receive their nestling freight, and are gone.

Our Master covers the fire, and snuffs out the candles
—don't you remember how daintily he used to pinch the
smoking wicks with forefinger and thumb, and then thrust
each hapless luminary head first into the tin socket ?—
and we waited for him.   The bells ring faintly in the
woods, over the hill in the valley.   They are gone.   The
school-house is dark and tenantless, and we are alone
with the night.

Merry, care-free company ! Some of them are sorrowing, some are dead, and all, I fear, are changed.   Spell !
Ah ! the "spell" that has come over that crowd of young
dreamers—over you, over me—will it ever, ever be
dissolved ? In the white radiance of Eternity !—*B. F.
Taylor.*

THE CHILDREN.

When the lessons and tasks are all ended,
    And the school for the day is dismissed,
And the little ones gather around me
    To bid me "good night" and be kissed ;
Oh, the little white arms that encircle
    My neck in a tender embrace !
Oh, the smiles that are halos of heaven,
    Shedding sunshine and love on my face !

And when they are gone I sit dreaming
Of my childhood, too lovely to last ;
Of love that my heart will remember
When it wakes to the pulse of the past,
Ere the world and its wickedness made me
A partner of sorrow and sin,
When the glory of God was about me
And the glory of gladness within.

Oh, my heart grows weak as a woman's
And the fountains of feeling will flow,
When I think of the paths steep and stony
Where the feet of the dear ones must go,
Of the mountains of sin hanging o'er them,
Of the tempest of fate blowing wild ;
Oh, there's nothing on earth half so holy
As the innocent heart of a child.

There are idols of hearts and of households,
They are angels of God in disguise,
His sunlight still sleeps in their tresses,
His glory still beams in their eyes ;
Oh, those truants from earth and from heaven,
They have made me more manly and mild,
And I know how Jesus could liken
The kingdom of God to a child.

Seek not a life for the dear ones,
All radiant as others have done,
But that life may have just as much shadow
To temper the glare of the sun ;
I would pray God to guard them from evil
But my prayer would bound back to myself;
Ah ! a seraph may pray for a sinner
But a sinner must pray for himself.

The twig is so easily bended,
   I have banished the rule and the rod ;
I have taught them the goodness of knowledge
   They have taught me the goodness of God.
My heart is a dungeon of darkness   ·
   Where I shut them from breaking a rule ;
My frown is sufficient correction
   My love is the law of the school.

I shall leave the old house in the autumn
   To traverse its threshold no more—
Ah, how I shall sigh for the dear ones
   That meet me each morn at the door.
I shall miss the good nights and the kisses,
   And the gush of their innocent glee,
The group on the green and the flowers
   That are brought every morn to me.

I shall miss them at morn and at eve,
   Their songs in the school and the street,
I shall miss the low hum of their voices,
   And the tramp of their delicate feet.
When the lesson and tasks are all ended,
   And death says the school is dismissed,
May the little ones gather around me
   To bid me "good night" and be kissed.
                              —*Charles Dickens.*

THE RAINY DAY.

The day is cold, and dark, and dreary ;
It rains and the wind is never weary ;
The vine still clings to the mouldering wall,
But at every gust the dead leaves fall,
And the day is dark and dreary.

My life is cold, and dark and dreary ;
It rains, and the wind is never weary ;
My thoughts still cling to the mouldering past,
But the hopes of youth fall thick in the blast,
And the days are dark and dreary.

Be still, sad heart ! and cease repining ;
Behind the clouds is the sun still shining ;
Thy fate is the common fate of all,
Into each life some rain must fall,
Some days must be dark and dreary..
—Longfellow.

MY SCHOOL-MATES.

The old school house is gone now, its site is vacant, and its play ground is silent as the memories that linger like ghosts of the departed around it. The joyous, juvenile host that once crowded its seats, or answered to the master's rat-tat on the window sash, are scattered to their sober tasks amidst the great working world, or lie resting with the dead.

My school-mates ! How memory struggles, with that word, to call back again the half-hundred sturdy boys and gleeful girls whose names stood with our own upon

the school roll ; to whom our boyhood owed so much of
its pleasures, and our manhood, perhaps, so much of its
character for good or evil.   As I am musing, slowly they
come around me again, and the old school room rings
again with the shouts of its merry population at their
noon time sports.   I mark again, in the reflected light of
a riper experience, the various traits and activities that
commended them to my school-boy regards, and read in
the magnified type of their manhood, the true value of
their childish virtues and vices.

And the first and saddest thought that presses upon
me, is the waste of intellect that has occurred amongst
them.   There were minds there, shrewd, capacious and
aspiring, for whom the parent or teacher had marked, in
the future, a career of high attainment or brilliant success.
Amongst that group of boys one might have marked the
embryo poets, scholars, statesmen, inventors and mer-
chants, the future men of thought and men of action, who
should fill the world with the blessings or the noise of
their achievements.   Bold, hardy, witty and free, strong
of will and stout hearted, there was in them the stuff of
which men are made.

Alas ! how few have fulfilled the promises of their
childhood.   The witty boy has become a dull, plodding
man.   The sparkling maiden is now but a nervous, nar-
row-minded woman.   The selfish demands of a selfish
world have fallen like a mildew upon the once free
thoughts.

Some are active business men, and "well to do," in the
world's phrase ; but who that knew them in the past
would not sigh to reflect how many generous, boyish
traits have been smothered to make them the men they
are ?

A few, and those not of the brightest, have more than
met the hopes we formed of them.   Generous, large

hearted men and women, they have but expanded into manly and womanly growth the good that dwelt in them in childhood. And it is a significant fact that it is the good far oftener than the bright child that has grown to be the successful, influential man. The trained heart has outrun the trained intellect in the race of life.—*Journal of Education.*

THE SMACK IN SCHOOL.

A *district* school not far away,
'Mid Berkshire hills, one winter's day,
Was humming with its wonted noise
Of three-score mingled girls and boys ;
Some few upon their tasks intent,
But more on furtive mischief bent.
The while the master's downward look
Was fastened on a copy-book ;
When suddenly, behind his back,
Rose sharp and clear a rousing smack !
As 'twere a battery of bliss
Let off in one tremendous kiss !
"What's that ?" the startled master cries ;
"That, thir," a little imp replies,
"Wath William Willith, if you pleath,
I thaw him kith Thuthanna Peathe !"
With a frown to make a statue thrill,
The master thundered, "Hither, Will !"
Like wretch o'ertaken in his track,
With stolen chattles on his back,
Will hung his head in fear and shame,
And to the awful presence came—
A great, green, bashful simpleton,
The butt of all good natured fun.

With smile suppressed, and birch upraised
The threatener faltered—"I'm amazed
That you, my biggest pupil, should
Be guilty of an act so rude !
Before the whole set school to boot—
What evil genius put you to't ?"
"'Twas she, herself, sir," sobbed the lad,
"I did not mean to be so bad ;
But when Susannah shook her curls,
And whispered, I was 'fraid of girls,
And dursn't kiss a baby's doll,
I couldn't stand it, sir, at all,
But up and kissed her on the spot !
I know—boo-hoo—I ought to not,
But, somehow, from her looks—boo-hoo—
I thought she kind o' wished me to !"—*Palmer*.

THE BRIDGE.

I stood on the bridge at midnight,
    As the clocks were striking the hour,
And the moon rose o'er the city,
    Behind the dark church-tower.

I saw her bright reflection
    In the water under me,
Like a golden goblet falling
    And sinking into the sea.

And far in the hazy distance
    Of that lovely night in June,
The blaze of the flaming furnace
    Gleamed redder than the moon.

Among the long, black rafters
The wavering shadows lay,
And the current that came from the ocean
Seemed to lift and bear then away ;

As, sweeping and eddying through them,
Rose the belated tide,
And streaming into the moonlight,
The seaweed floated wide.

And like those waters rushing
Among the wooden piers,
A flood of thoughts came o'er me
That filled my eyes with tears.

How often, O how often,
In the days that had gone by,
I had stood on that bridge at midnight
And gazed on that wave and sky !

How often, O how often,
I had wished that the ebbing tide
Would bear me away on its bosom
O'er the ocean wild and wide !

For my heart was hot and restless,
And my life was full of care,
And the burden laid upon me
Seemed greater than I could bear.

But now it has fallen from me,
It is buried in the sea ;
And only the sorrow of others
Throws its shadow over me.

Yet whenever I cross the river
  On its bridge with wooden piers,
Like the odor of brine from the ocean,
  Comes the thought of other years.

And I think how many thousands
  Of care-encumbered men,
Each bearing his burden of sorrow,
  Have crossed the bridge since then.

I see the long procession
  Still passing to and fro,
The young heart hot and restless,
  And the old subdued and slow !

And forever and forever,
  As long as the river flows,
As long as the heart has passions,
  As long as life has woes ;

The moon and its broken reflection
  And its shadows shall appear,
As the symbol of love in heaven,
  And its wavering image here.—*Longfellow.*

SELECT THOUGHTS.

He who has lost his honor can lose nothing more.

Charms strike the sight, but merit wins the soul.—*Pope.*

The truest end of life is to know the life that never ends.—*Penn.*

The man who minds his own business has a good, steady employment.

Evil is wrought by want of thought as well as by want of heart.—*Hood.*

Would you have others speak highly of you ? Never speak highly of yourself.

To most men experience is like the stern lights of a ship, which illumine only the track it has passed.— *Coleridge.*

Would you have fame ? Write your name in deeds of kindness, love and mercy on the hearts you come in contact with.

The bright days of youth are the. seed time of life. Every action is a seed whose good or evil fruit will be the happiness or misery of after life.

It is not money, nor is it mere intellect, that governs the world ; it is moral character ; it is intellect associated with moral excellence.—*T. D. Woolsey.*

> Vice is a monster of such hideous mien,
> That to be hated needs but to be seen ;
> Yet seen too oft, familiar with her face,
> We first endure, then pity, then embrace.

> > Unto the one who labors,
> > Fearless of foe or frown ;
> > Unto the kindly hearted
> > Cometh a blessing down.
> > > —*Mary Francis Tyler.*

The mind is the man.—*Tyrtæus.*

The mind only is true wealth.—*Adolph of Nassau.*

We live not in body but in mind.—*Speusippus.*

A good mind is a kingdom in itself.—*R. Leighton.*

A vacant mind is an invitation to vice.—*B. Gilpin.*

Every duty we omit obscures some truth we should have known.—*Ruskin.*

The line of life is a ragged diagonal between duty and desire.—*W. R. Alger.*

When any calamity has been suffered the first thing to be remembered is how much has been escaped.—*Johnson.*

A loving heart and a pleasant countenance are commodities which a man should never fail to take home with him.

Every lie, great or small, is the brink of a precipice, the depth of which nothing but Omniscience can fathom.—*Reade.*

> And when the world shall link your name
>   With gracious lives and manners fine,
> The teacher shall assert her claims,
>   And proudly whisper, "These were mine."
>   —*Whittier.*

If vexed with a child when instructing it, try to write with your left hand.   Remember a child is all left-handed.—*J. F. Boyes.*

I can easier teach twenty what were good to be done than be one of the twenty to follow my own teaching.—*Shakespeare.*

Instructors should not only be skillful in those sciences which they teach, but have skill in the method of teaching and patience in the practice.—*Dr. Watts.*

We often praise the evening clouds,
And tints so gay and bold,
But seldom think upon our God
Who tinged the clouds with gold.—*Scott.*

It is because all ties must part
That farewell words are spoken.—*Robert Wilson.*

Sweet is the love that nature brings.—*Wadsworth.*

Nothing pays that's wrong,
The good and pure alone are sure
To bring prolonged success.—*Anon.*

Grace is to the body, what good sense is to the mind.
—*Franklin.*

Those who would make us feel must feel themselves.
--*Churchill.*

Men should prove by their doing the correctness of
their living.—*Anon.*

THE DESTRUCTION OF SENNACHERIB.

The Assyrian came down like the wolf on the fold,
And his cohorts were gleaming in purple and gold ;
And the sheen of their spears was like stars on the sea,
When the blue wave rolls nightly on deep Galilee.

Like the leaves of the forest when summer is green,
That host with their banners at sunset were seen ;
Like the leaves of the forest when autumn hath blown,
That host on the morrow lay withered and strown.

For the Angel of Death spread his wings on the blast ;
And breathed in the face of the foe as he passed ;
And the eyes of the sleepers waxed deadly and chill
And their hearts but once heaved, and forever grew still ;

And there lay the steed with his nostrils all wide,
But through it there roll'd not the breath of his pride,
And the foam of his gasping lay white on the turf,
And cold as the spay of the rock-beating surf.

And there lay the rider, distorted and pale, .
With the dew on his brow and the rust on his mail ;
And the tents were all silent, the banners alone,
The lances unlifted, the trumpet unblown.

And the widows of Ashur are loud in their wail,
And the idols are broke in the temple of Baal ;
And the might of the Gentile, unsmote by the sword,
Hath melted like snow in the glance of the Lord !

—Byron.

"THE OLD ARM CHAIR."

I love it, I love it, and who shall dare
To chide me for loving the "Old Arm Chair ?"
I've treasur'd it long as a holy prize,
I've bedew'd it with tears and embalmed it with sighs ;
'Tis bound by a thousand bands to my heart ;
Not a tie will break, not a link will start.
Would you learn the spell ?—a mother sat there,
And a sacred thing is that "Old Arm Chair."

In childhood's home, I lingered near
The hallow'd seat, with list'ning ear,
And gentle words did mother give
To fit me to die, and teach me to live ;
She told me shame would never betide,
With truth for my creed and God for my guide ;
She taught me to lisp my earliest prayer
As I knelt beside that "Old Arm Chair."

I sat and watched for many a day
When her eyes grew dim, and her locks were gray,
And I almost worship'd her when she smiled,
And turned from her Bible to bless her child.
Years rolled on, but the last one sped—
My idol was shattered, my earth-star fled.
I learned how much the heart can bear
When I saw her die in the "Old Arm Chair."

'Tis past, 'tis past, but I gaze on it now
With quivering breath and throbbing brow ;
'T was there she nursed me, 'twas there she died,
And memory flows with lava tide.
Say it is folly and deem me weak,
While the scalding drops start down my cheek ;
But I love it, I love it, and can not tear
My soul from a mother's "Old Arm Chair."

—Eliza Cook.

THE MOTHER BIRD.

"Peep, peep, peep !" says she ;
"One, two, three, one, two, three
Little birds who wait for me !

"One is yellow, two are brown,
And their throats are soft with down ;
On each head a scarlet crown.

"Mother-bird is flying fast ;
Soon your hunger will be past ;
Here is mother, come at last.

"Peep, peep, peep !" says she ;
"And can it be ?—ah ! can it be ?
No little ones are here for me."

In vain her cry, in vain her quest,
A thoughtless boy has robbed her nest ;
She looks around with aching breast.

Nursery.

VENTILATION AND TEMPERATURE.

First in order of importance is ventilation. The school must have a steady supply of fresh air throughout the day. The symptoms which indicate neglect of this are very plain. Perhaps the teacher may often be conscious of a dimness of eyesight, a giddiness of head, a general languor and drowsiness, which nothing can shake off, and for which she cannot well account : it is probable that they are largely owing to her working in impure air. Many continue even to bear headaches, sickness, or sore throat, without ever suspecting that these are owing to the same cause. If such be the effect on the teacher, is it to be supposed that the children will escape? Their countenances and the tones of their voice are some index to the state of the school. And if the teacher will scruti- nize these, as she should accustom herself to do, she will be kept from error in this matter. It is not enough that the air be fresh in the morning, or that the windows be opened and closed fitfully throughout the day, just as ac- cident may direct her attention to the subject, or that there be one stereotyped degree of ventilation throughout the year. This is a matter that requires attention from hour to hour, and from day to day, according to wind and weather. An atmosphere which is fresh in the morning very soon becomes vitiated unless it is changed, and the teacher may not be conscious of its condition. Nothing but constant watchfulness will suffice to maintain the air in proper condition. During the recess the windows should be opened, and the school-room thoroughly aired.

Another important feature is the keeping up of a proper degree of temperature in the school-room. Both ex- tremes of temperature must be avoided. If the tempera- ture be kept habitually too high, the children will become nervously sensitive of cold. At the same time the air may be fresh, and yet injuriously cold. Particularly are drafts to be avoided. As many schools are constructed, it is hardly possible to avoid these. A class should not stand immediately under an open window or behind a door. A thermometer should be provided for each school-room ; and should be hung in the middle of the room, and examined by the teacher once an hour at least, while the heating apparatus is in operation. Sixty-eight degrees Fahrenheit should be the maximum temperature of the school-room, although seventy degrees is not ob- jectionable during the first half hour of the session in very cold weather.—*Superintendent McAlister in the Teacher.*

NOBODY'S CHILD.

Alone in the dreary, pitiless street,
With my torn old dress, and bare, cold feet,
All day I have wandered to and fro,
Hungry and shivering, and nowhere to go ;
The night's coming on in darkness and dread,
And the chill sleet beating upon my bare head.
Oh ! why does the wind blow upon me so wild !
Is it because I am nobody's child ?

Just over the way there's a flood of light,
And warmth and beauty, and all things bright ;
Beautiful children, in robes so fair,
Are caroling songs in their rapture there,
I wonder if they, in their blissful glee,
Would pity a poor little beggar like me,
Wandering alone in the merciless street,
Naked and shivering and nothing to eat ?

Oh ! what shall I do when the night comes down,
In its terrible blackness, all over the town ?
Shall I lay me down 'neath the angry sky,
On the cold, hard pavement alone to die,
When the beautiful children their prayers have said,
And their mammas have tucked them up snugly in bed?
For no dear mother on *me* ever smiled,
Why is it, I wonder, I'm nobody's child ?

No father, no mother, no sister, not one
In all the world loves me ; e'en the little dogs run
When I wander too near them ; 'tis wondrous to see,
How everything shrinks from a beggar like me !

Perhaps 'tis a dream ; but sometimes, when I lie
Gazing far up in the dark blue sky,
Watching for hours some large, bright star,
I fancy the beautiful gates are ajar,
And a host of white-robed, nameless things,
Come fluttering o'er me on gilded wings ;
A hand that is strangely soft and fair
Caresses gently my tangled hair,
And a voice like the carol of some wild bird—
The sweetest voice that was ever heard—
Calls me many a dear, pet name,
Till my heart and spirit are all aflame.

They tell me of such unbounded love,
And bid me come up to their home above ;
And then, with such pitiful, sad surprise,
They look at me with their sweet, tender eyes ;
And it seems to me, out of the dreary night ;
I am going up to that world of light ;
And, away from the hunger and storm so wild,
I am sure I shall then be somebody's child.

                              —*Phila H. Case*,

THE GRAVE.

The sorrow for the dead is the only sorrow from which
we refuse to be divorced.   Every other wound we seek to
heal ; every other affliction, to forget ; but this wound,
we consider it a duty to keep open.   This affliction we
cherish, and brood over in solitude.   Where is the mother,
who would willingly forget the infant that has perished

like a blossom from her arms, though every recollection is a pang ? Where is the child, that would willingly forget a tender parent, though to remember be but to lament ? Who, even in the hour of agony, would forget the friend, over whom he mourns ?

No, the love which survives the tomb, is one of the noblest attributes of the soul. If it has its woes, it has likewise its delights ; and when the overwhelming burst of grief is calmed into the gentle tear of recollection ; when the sudden anguish, and the convulsive agony over the present ruins of all that we most loved, is softened away into pensive meditation on all that it was, in the days of its loveliness, who would root out such a sorrow from the heart ? Though it may, sometimes, throw a passing cloud over the bright hour of gayety, or spread a deeper sadness over the hour of gloom, yet, who would exchange it, even for the song of pleasure, or the burst of revelry ? No, there is a voice from the tomb sweeter than song. There is a remembrance of the dead, to which we turn, even from the charms of the living.

Oh, the grave ! the grave ! It buries every error, covers every defect, extinguishes every resentment ! From its peaceful bosom, spring none but fond regrets and tender recollections. Who can look down upon the grave, even of an enemy, and not feel a compunctious throb, that he should have warred with the poor handful of earth that lies mouldering before him ? But the grave of those we loved, what a place for meditation ! There it is, that we call up, in long review, the whole history of virtue and gentleness, and the thousand endearments lavished upon us, almost unheeded, in the daily intercourse of intimacy ; there it is, that we dwell upon the tenderness, the solemn, awful tenderness of the parting scene ; the bed of death, with all its stifled griefs, its noiseless attendance, its mute, watchful assiduities ! the last testimonies of expiring love! the feeble, fluttering, thrilling,—oh, how thrilling!—pressure of the hand! the last fond look of the glazing eye turned upon us, even from the threshold of existence! the faint, faltering accents, struggling in death to give one more assurance of affection!

Ay, go to the grave of buried love and meditate! There settle the account with thy conscience, for every past benefit unrequited; every past endearment unregarded, of that departed being, who can never—never—never return to be soothed by thy contrition! If thou art a child, and hast ever added a sorrow to the soul, or a furrow to the silvered brow of an affectionate parent; if thou art a husband, and hast ever caused the fond bosom that ventured its whole happiness in thy arms, to doubt one moment of thy kindness or thy truth; if thou art a friend, and hast ever wronged, in thought, or word, or deed, the spirit that generously confided in thee; if thou hast given one unmerited pang to that true heart, which now lies cold and still beneath thy feet; then be sure, that every unkind look, every ungracious word, every ungentle action, will come thronging back upon thy memory, and knocking dolefully at thy soul; then be sure, that thou wilt lie down sorrowing and repentant on the grave, and utter the unheard groan, and pour the unavailing tear; more deep, more bitter, because unheard and unavailing.

Then weave thy chaplet of flowers, and strew the beauties of nature about the grave; console thy broken spirit, if thou canst, with these tender, yet futile tributes of regret; but take warning, by the bitterness of this, thy contrite affliction over the dead, and henceforth be more faithful and affectionate in the discharge of thy duties to the living.—*W. Irving.*

A PSALM OF LIFE.

Tell me not in mournful numbers,
　　Life is but an empty dream !
For the soul is dead that slumbers,
　　And things are not what they seem.

Life is real ! Life is earnest !
　　And the grave is not its goal ;
Dust thou art, to dust returnest,
　　Was not written of the soul.

Not enjoyment, and not sorrow,
　　Is our destined end and way,
But to act, that each to-morrow
　　Find us further than to-day.

Art is long, and time is fleeting,
　　And our hearts, though stout and brave,
Still, like muffled drums, are beating
　　Funeral marches to the grave.

In the world's broad field of battle,
　　In the bivouac of life,
Be not like dumb, driven cattle,
　　Be a hero in the strife !

Trust not Future, howe'er pleasant !
　　Let the dead Past bury its dead !
Act !—act in the living Present !
　　Heart within, and God o'er head.

Lives of great men all remind us
　　We can make our lives sublime,
And, departing, leave behind us
　　Footprints on the sands of time ;

Footprints, that perhaps another,
　Sailing o'er life's solemn main,
A forlorn and shipwreck'd brother,
　Seeing, shall take heart again.

Let us, then, be up and doing,
　With a heart for any fate ;
Still achieving, still pursuing,
　Learn to labor and to wait.
                    —*H. W. Longfellow.*

AFTER MARRIAGE.

Enter LADY TEAZLE *and* SIR PETER.

Sir P.　Lady Teazle, Lady Teazle, I'll not bear it.

Lady T.　Sir Peter, Sir Peter, you may bear it or not, as you please ; but I ought to have my own way in everything, and, what's more, I will too.　What ! though I was educated in the country, I know very well that women of fashion in London are accountable to nobody after they are married.

Sir P.　Very well, ma'am, very well ; so a husband is to have no influence—no authority ?

Lady T.　Authority ! No to be sure.　If you. wanted authority over me you should have adopted me, and not married me ; I am sure you were old enough.

Sir P.　Old enough ! ay—there it is.　Well, well, Lady Teazle, though my life may be made unhappy by your temper, I'll not be ruined by your extravagance.

Lady T.　My extravagance ! I am sure I am not more extravagant than a woman ought to be.

Sir P.　No, no, madam, you shall throw away no more sums upon such unmeaning luxury.　'Slife ! to spend as much to furnish your dressing-room with flowers in winter as would suffice to turn the Pantheon into a green-house.

Lady T. Sir Peter, am I to blame because flowers are dear in cold weather? You should find fault with the climate, and not with me. For my part, I'm sure, I wish it were spring all the year round, and that roses grew under our feet.

Sir P. Zounds! madam, if you had been born to this, I should not wonder at your talking thus; but you forget what your situation was when I married you.

Lady T.· No, no, I don't; 'twas a very disagreeable one, or I should never have married you.

Sir P. Yes, yes, madam; you were then in a somewhat humbler style—the daughter of a plain country squire. Recollect, Lady Teazle, when I saw you first sitting at your tambour, in a pretty-figured linen gown, with a bunch of keys at your side—your hair combed smooth over a roll, and your apartment hung round with fruits in worsted of your own working.

Lady T. Oh yes, I remember it very well; and a curious life I led. My daily occupation, to inspect the dairy, superintend the poultry, make extracts from the family receipt-book and comb my Aunt Deborah's lap-dog.

Sir P. Yes, yes, ma'am 'twas so indeed.

Lady T. And then, you know, my evening amusements—to draw patterns for ruffles which I had not material to make up, to play Pope Juan with the curate, to read a novel to my aunt, or to be stuck down to an old spinet to strum my father to sleep after a fox-chase.

Sir P. I am glad you have so good a memory. Yes, madam, these were the recreations I took you from; but now you must have your coach—vis-a-vis—and three powdered footmen before your chair, and, in the summer, a pair of white cats to draw you to Kensington Gardens. No recollection, I suppose, when you were content to ride double, behind the butler, on a docked coach-horse !

Lady T. No, I swear I never did that ; I deny the butler and the coach-horse.

Sir P. This, madam, was your situation, and what have I done for you ? I have made you a woman of fashion, of fortune, of rank ; in short, I have made you my wife.

Lady T. Well, then—and there is but one thing more you can make me add to the obligation, and that is—

Sir P. My widow, I suppose ?

Lady T. Hem ! hem !

Sir P. I thank you, madam ; but don't flatter yourself; for, though your ill-conduct may disturb my peace of mind, it shall never break my heart, I promise you. However, I am equally obliged to you for the hint.

Lady T. Then why will you endeavor to make yourself so disagreeable to me, and thwart me in every little elegant expense ?

Sir P. 'Slife ! madam, I say, had you any of these little elegant expenses when you married me ?

Lady T. Lud ! Sir Peter, would you have me be out of the fashion ?

Sir P. The fashion, indeed ! What had you to do with the fashion before you married me !

Lady T. For my part, I should think you would like to have your wife thought a woman of taste.

Sir P. Ay—there again—taste ! Zounds ! madam, you had no taste when you married me !

Lady T. That's very true, indeed, Sir Peter ; and, after having married you, I should never pretend to taste again, I allow. (*Laughs.*) But now, Sir Peter, since we have finished our daily jangle, I presume I may go to my engagement at Lady Sneerwell's.

Sir P. Ay, there's another precious circumstance— a charming set of acquaintance you have made there.

Lady T. Nay, Sir Peter, they are all people of rank and fortune, and remarkably tenacious of reputation.

Sir P. Yes, egad, they are tenacious of reputation with a vengeance, for they don't choose any body should have a character but themselves. Such a crew! Ah! many a wretch has rid on a hurdle who has done less mischief than these utterers of forged tales, coiners of scandal, and clippers of reputation.

Lady T. What! would you restrain the freedom of speech?

Sir P. Ah! they have made you just as bad as any one of the society.

Lady T. Why, I believe I do bear a part with a tolerable grace.

Sir P. Grace, indeed!

Lady T. But I vow I bear no malice against the people I abuse. When I say an ill-natured thing, 'tis out of pure good humor, and I take it for granted they deal exactly in the same manner with me. But, Sir Peter, you know you promised to come to Lady Sneerwell's too.

Sir P. Well, well, I'll call in just to look after my own character.

Lady T. Then, indeed, you must make haste after me, or you'll be too late. So good-by to ye. [*Exit.*

Sir P. So I have gained much by my intended expostulation; yet with what a charming air she contradicts everything I say, and how pleasingly she shows her contempt for my authority! Well, though I can't make her love me, there is great satisfaction in quarreling with her; and I think she never appears to such advantage as when she is doing everything in her power to plague me. [*Exit.*]   —*R. B. Sheridan.*

MODULATION.

'T is not enough the *voice* be sound and clear,
'T is *modulation* that must charm the ear.
When desperate heroes grieve with tedious moan,
And whine their sorrows in a see-saw tone,
The same soft sounds of unimpassioned woes,
Can only make the yawning hearers doze.
The voice all modes of passion can express,
That marks the proper word with proper stress ;
But none emphatic can that speaker call,
Who lays an *equal* emphasis on *all.*

Some o'er the tongue the labored measures roll,
Slow and deliberate as the parting toll ;
Point every stop, mark every pause so strong,
Their words like stage processions stalk along.

All affectation but creates disgust ;
And e'en in *speaking,* we may seem too just.
In vain for *them* the pleasing measure flows,
Whose recitation runs it all to prose ;
Repeating what the poet sets not down,
The verb disjointing from its favorite noun,
While pause, and break, and repetition join
To make a discord in each tuneful line.

Some placid natures fill the allotted scene
With lifeless drawls, insipid and serene ;
While *others* thunder every couplet o'er,
And almost crack your ears with rant and roar.
More nature oft, and finer strokes are shown
In the low whisper, than tempestuous tone ;

And Hamlet's hollow voice and fixed amaze,
More powerful terror to the mind conveys,
Than he, who, swollen with impetuous rage,
Bullies the bulky phantom of the stage.

He who, in earnest, studies o'er his part,
Will find true nature cling about his heart.
The modes of grief are not included all
In the white handkerchief and mournful drawl ;
A single *look* more marks the internal woe,
Than all the windings of the lengthened *Oh !*
Up to the face the quick sensation flies,
And darts its meaning from the speaking eyes :
Love, transport, madness, anger, scorn, despair,
And all the passions, all the soul is there.—*Lloyd.*

www.ingramcontent.com/pod-product-compliance
Lightning Source LLC
Chambersburg PA
CBHW020252290326
41930CB00039B/1028